www.**free-fudge-download**.com
& other foodie fantasies

Published by MQ Publications Limited
12 The Ivories, 6–8 Northampton Street, London N1 2HY
Tel: 020 7359 2244 / Fax: 020 7359 1616
email: mail@mqpublications.com

Copyright © Lisa Swerling and Ralph Lazar 2003
Published under exclusive licence by MQ Publications Ltd
The moral rights of the authors have been asserted

ISBN: 1-84072-516-8

3 5 7 9 0 8 6 4 2

Printed and bound in Italy

www.free-fudge-download.com

& other foodie fantasies

BY LISA SWERLING & RALPH LAZAR

MQP

ACTIVATING THE ULTIMATE TOASTER

CHILDHOOD DREAMS:
DISCOVERING THE LEGENDARY JELLYBEAN ANT COLONY

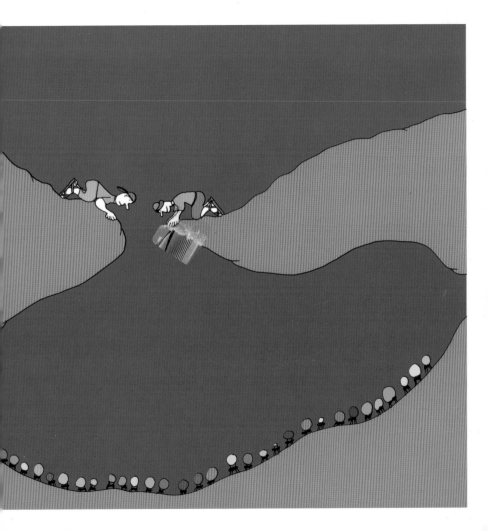

THE SUSHI THAT GOT AWAY

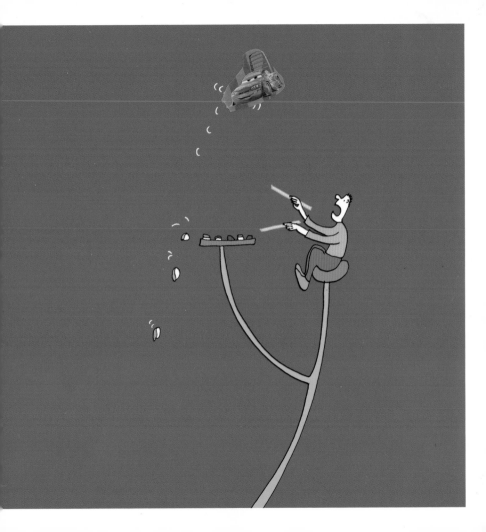

THE MARVELLOUS COMPULSIVENESS OF PISTACHIO NUTS

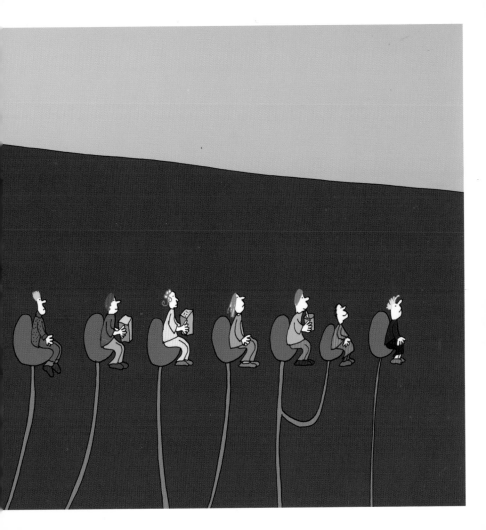

homemade vegetable soup

ONION CABBAGE SPINACH

THE FUEL OF NEW YORK CITY...
BAGELS
SUSHI
PASTA
NOODLES
HAMBURGERS
ICED TEA
PICKLES
CREAM

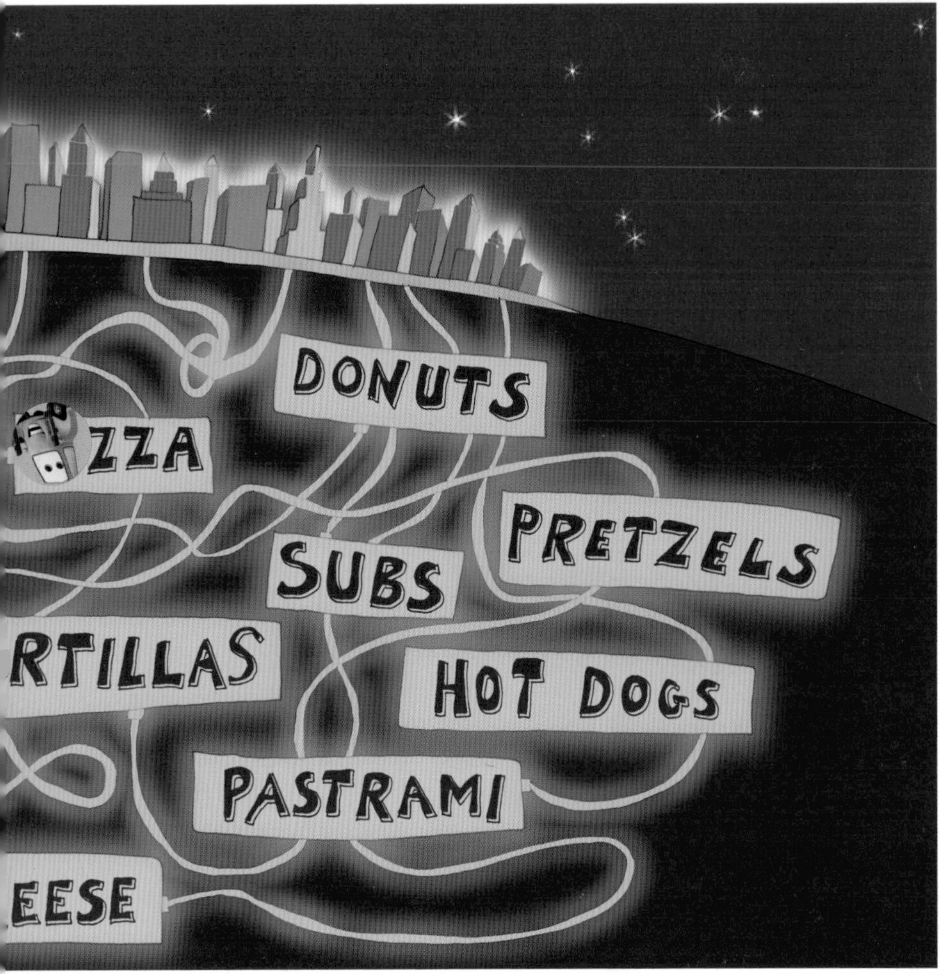

DONUTS
ZZA
PRETZELS
SUBS
RTILLAS
HOT DOGS
PASTRAMI
EESE

NOTHING LIKE A GOOD FAMILY BARBEQUE

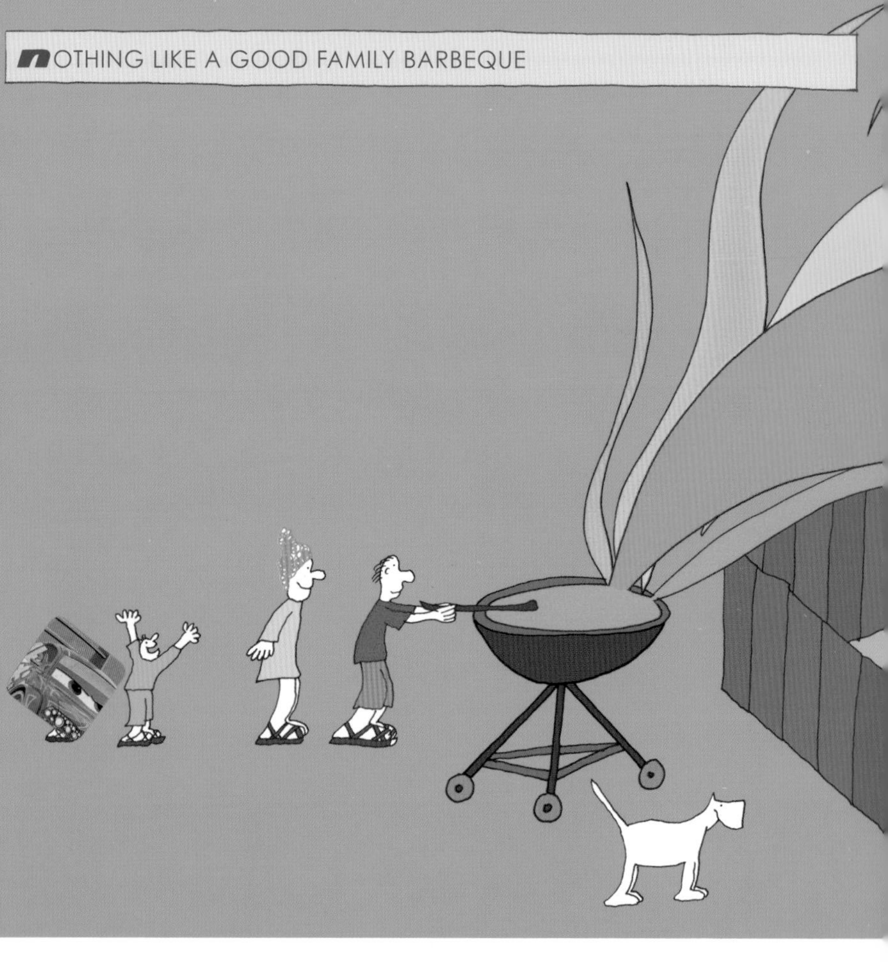

FRIENDSHIP IS THE WINE OF LIFE

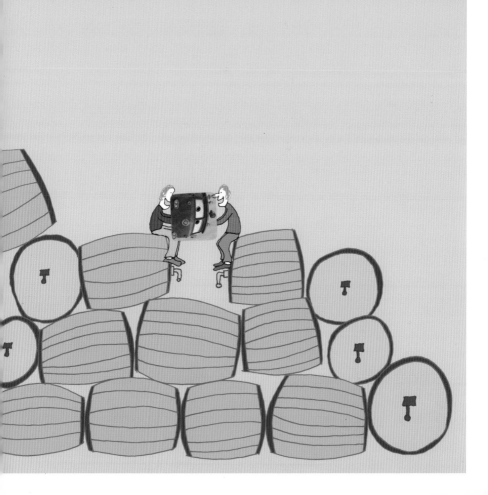

Keep your eyes on the sidewalk!
Watch where you're going egg-head!
LUIGI'S PASTA HOUSE
YIN + YANG NOODLES

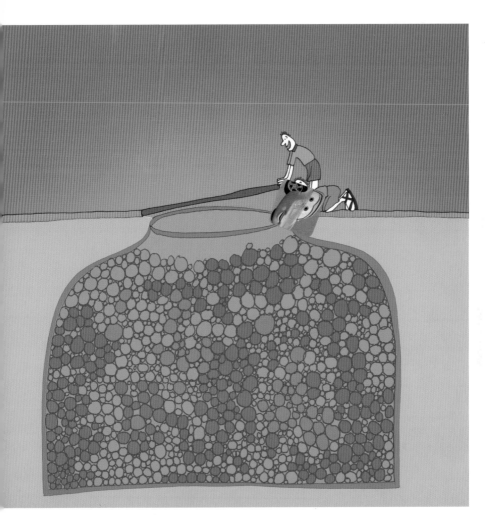

dINNER PARTY DISASTERS: FIRST ATTEMPT AT RADISH AND CURRIED APPLE SOUP

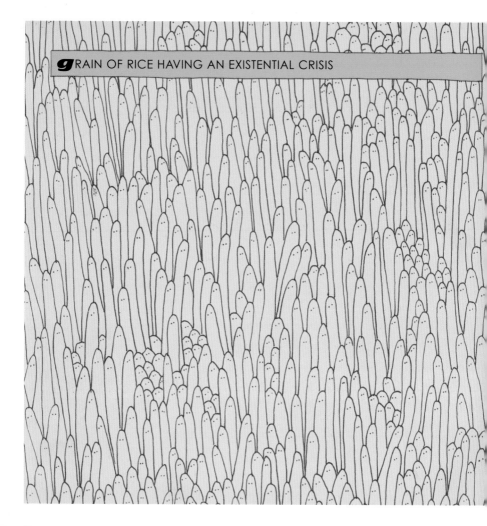

gRAIN OF RICE HAVING AN EXISTENTIAL CRISIS

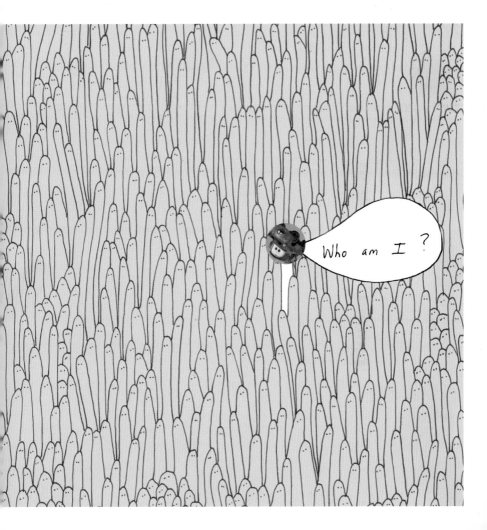

THE WARM GLOW OF COMFORT FOOD

BE PREPARED FOR WHEN THE DONUT RAINS COME

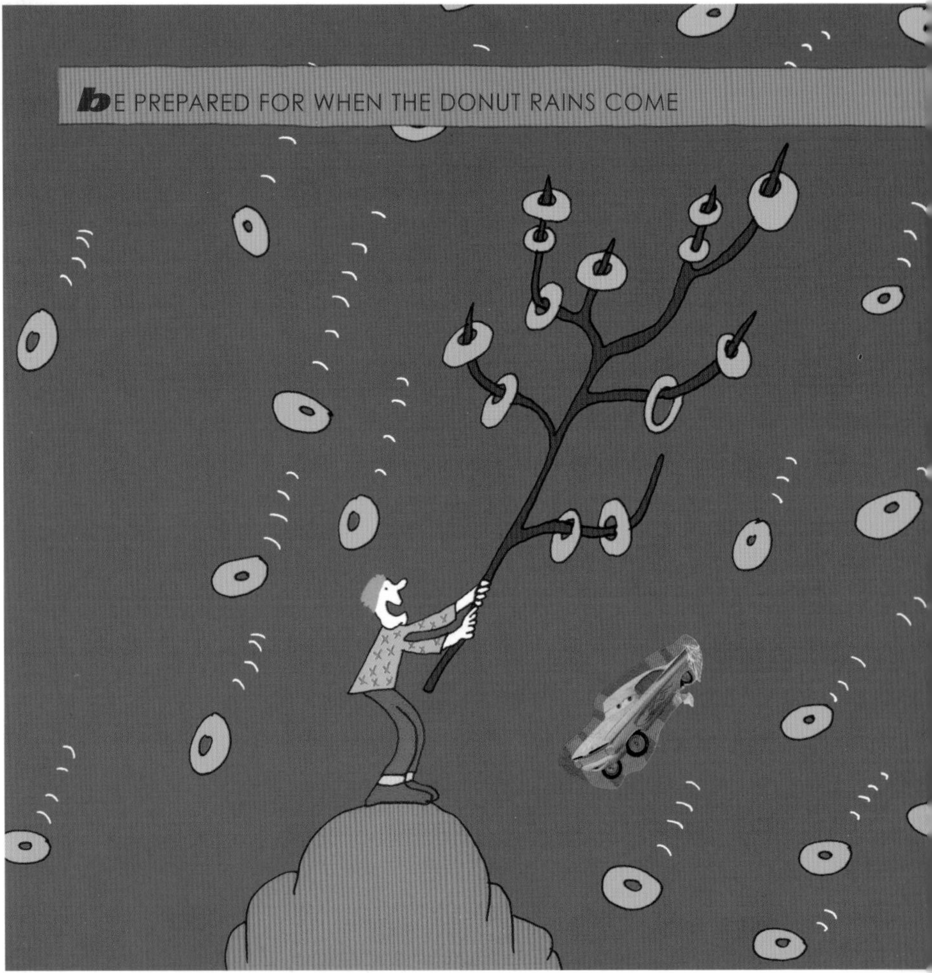

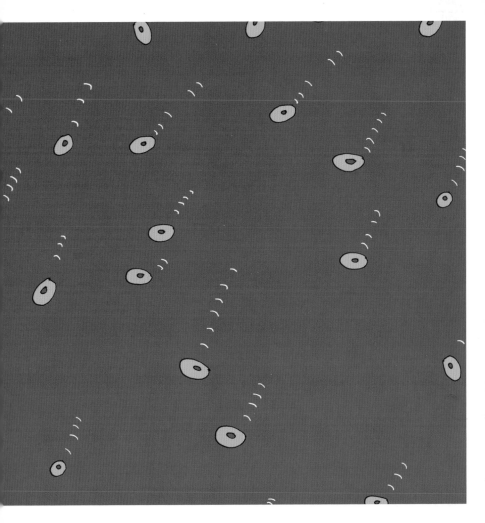

GOOD TIMES AT THE FAT-FREE, LOW-CARB CAFFEINE-FREE CAFE

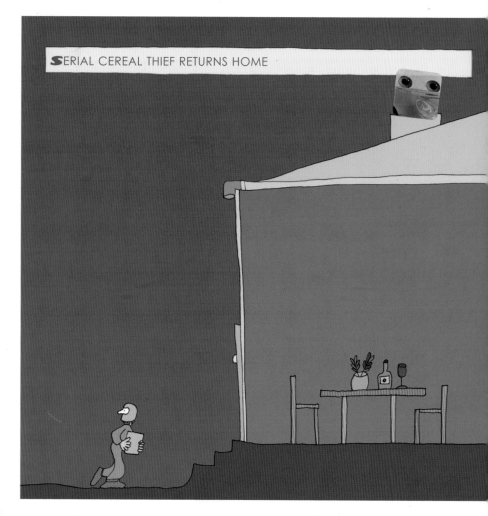

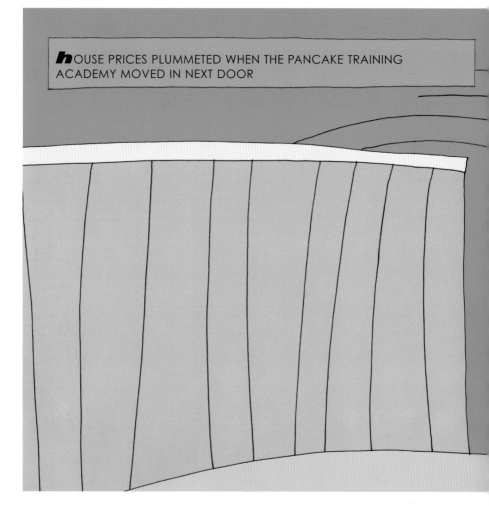

*h*OUSE PRICES PLUMMETED WHEN THE PANCAKE TRAINING ACADEMY MOVED IN NEXT DOOR

THE SECRET-DINNER-SIPHON (S-D-S): USED TO GET RID OF THE MAIN COURSE, TO LEAVE ROOM FOR DESSERT

ABOUT THE AUTHORS

Ralph Lazar and Lisa Swerling are
currently based in the UK. Their other
series include *Harold's Planet* and *Epsilon
Osborne, hero of the corporate jungle*.